ALIENS
JOKE BOOK

Colin and Jacqui Hawkins

An imprint of HarperCollins*Publishers*

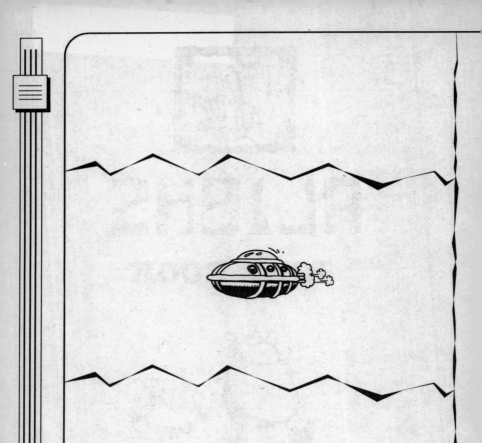

First published in Great Britain by Collins Picture Books in 2001

1 3 5 7 9 10 8 6 4 2

ISBN: 0 00 710854 0

Text and illustrations copyright © HarperCollins Publishers Ltd

Thanks to Karl Richardson of Advocate for artwork.

The HarperCollins website address is: www.fireandwater.com

Printed and bound in Great Britain by
Omnia Books Limited, Glasgow

CONTENTS

They're out there! In another part of the Universe, zooming from planet to planet in search of... er... whatever it is they're in search of, the intrepid crew of the *ZS Rambler* flash through space, finding themselves in all sorts of scrapes.

Hot on the *Rambler's* tail is the *Intergalactic Zoo*, the fearsome Zoomaster at the helm, with one thing on his mind — how to get his clutches on Lugg and the others aboard the *Rambler*, and put them in the cage reserved specially for them in the *Intergalactic Zoo*.

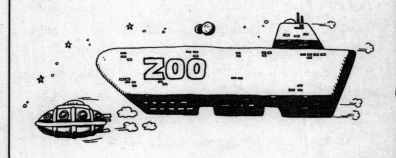

And what a fine assortment of aliens they are!

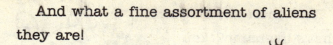

There's Glich, a formidable figure of an alien, her four fingers firmly on the controls, her beady eye (all one of it) fixed on the space ahead!

There's Lugg, an Amazon of an alien, with hair a fetching shade of orange. A mechanical genius, she knows precisely how to deal with a splattered sprocket, a twisted tube, an exhausted exhaust and all the other things that can go wrong with an engine as complex as the *ZS Rambler's* – and what she can do with a safety pin is nobody's business!

Then there's... er... er... what's-his-name? You know! The one with four eyes and the longest tongue in the universe. Derek, is it? No, not

Derek! Dekko. Long in vision, but a bit short in the old memory stakes.

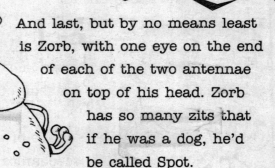

And last, but by no means least is Zorb, with one eye on the end of each of the two antennae on top of his head. Zorb has so many zits that if he was a dog, he'd be called Spot.

And what do they do they do when they're off duty?

They tell jokes.

So, zip up your spacesuit, clamber up the steps and get ready to blast-off on a fun-filled voyage to new worlds of laughter.

Every night before they turn in, the crew of the *ZS Rambler* fill in the ship's log, a record of the events that occur each day. Here are some of the entries for a recent spin round a solar system in the Garbagia galaxy, first left past Fido (the Doggy star) and straight on till lunchtime...

▶ **STARDATE 000.001**

The *ZS Rambler* passed Planet Antarctica, a place where the temperature never rises above freezing. Zorb reported that he saw an Antarctican with his nose in a book.

'What was he reading?' Glich asked.

'A Penguin paperback!' replied Zorb.

STARDATE 000.002

Flew through an electrical storm that sent all the ship's instruments, apart from the calculator, barmy. That's the good thing about calculators – you can always count on them.

STARDATE 000.003

Medical records updated to show that Zorb complained that he had acid indigestion after lunch – his own fault for putting so much acid on his fish and chips!

STARDATE 000.004

ZS Rambler forced to land on a planet that is overrun by ants. Some of them were so small you could hardly see them. 'These are the inf-ants,' said Zorb, consulting his *Tough Guide to the Universe*. No sooner had he said it than an enormous ant appeared on the horizon. 'Run!' shouted Zorb. 'That's a gi-ant!'

The ants, it is reported, turned out to be really friendly, apart from their leader who bullied everyone to get his own way.

'He's such a tyr-ant!' sighed one little bug.

Left the ant planet, but about twenty minutes after take-off, found two stowaway ants who had runaway to get married.

'Let them stay,' smiled Glich. 'They're harmless ant-elopers!'

'Do you know,' said Zorb at breakfast, taking a bite out of a piece of fruit, 'that an apple a day keeps the doctor at bay.'

'How?' asked Dekko.

'Well,' grinned Zorb. 'You take careful aim and fire!'

STARDATE 000.008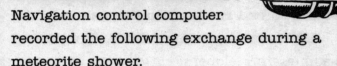

Navigation control computer recorded the following exchange during a meteorite shower.

'This ship's like a baby,' cried Lugg struggling to control the ship as it shook from side to side.

'What do you mean?' shouted Dekko.

'It won't go anywhere without a rattle!'

STARDATE 000.009

Lugg recorded her astonishment at seeing a wizard on a broomstick whizz past the ZS Rambler.

'Don't worry,' giggled Glich. 'It's only a flying sorceror!'

The *ZS Rambler* flew past a planet orbited by a huge, shining moon. 'That's the stupidest moon I've ever seen,' said Zorb.

'Why's that?' asked Dekko.

'Because it's a fool moon,' giggled Zorb.

 STARDATE 000.011

Lugg logged her intention to land the *ZS Rambler* on Planet Megabright but later recorded that she had been unable to do so.

'I hovered for hours,' she notes, 'but still couldn't find a parking meteor!'

 STARDATE 000.012 ⬇ **EXTRACT FROM VOICE RECORDER**

'Look!' cried Dekko, pointing through the porthole. 'What's that eggy-looking thing overtaking us?'

'Don't worry,' laughed Lugg. 'It's only an Unidentified Frying Object!'

'I want to go to the ladies!' said Dekko, after breakfast.

'The ladies!' the rest of the crew gasped. 'But you're a male!'

'I know,' said Dekko. 'But I want to be like Captain Kirk!'

'What's that got to do with going to the ladies?' asked Glich.

'Because he boldly goes where no man has gone before!'

STARDATE 000.014

Dekko recorded seeing Mickey Mouse on a space walk. Apparently he was looking for Pluto!

'Think it's time I went on a diet,' sighed Glich, rubbing her tummy after supper one night.

'Yes,' agreed Zorb. 'You are beginning to look like an extra-cholesterol!'

STARDATE 000.016

It is recorded that a solar flare from a sun in the constellation Burgerbar sent the *ZS Rambler* way off course, forcing it to land on Earth. 'Put on something warm,' said Dekko. 'I think we've come down in a cold spot.'

'What makes you think that?' asked Zorb.

'There's a sign over there,' said Dekko. 'It says, Welcome to Chile!'

Must report that the *ZS Rambler* was damaged when it landed on Earth, and the crew decided to go on a whirlwind world tour whilst the ship was repaired. Their first stop was Venice. 'I wonder how you make a Venetian blind,' said Lugg.

'Simple,' said Zorb. 'You stick a finger in his eye!'

> **STARDATE 000.018**

EXTRACT FROM VOICE RECORDER

LOCATION: OSLO, NORWAY.

Lugg: I want to ask that man the way to the Royal Palace, but I don't speak Norwegian.

Dekko: I know what to do.

Lugg: What?

Dekko: Use the Norse Code!

STARDATE 000.019

EXTRACT FROM
VOICE RECORDER

LOCATION: LONDON, ENGLAND.

Glich: Look at that man over there.
He's got outer space teeth.

Lugg: What do you mean, outer space
teeth?

Glich: Full of black holes!

STARDATE 000.020

EXTRACT FROM
VOICE RECORDER

Lugg: (glancing through a porthole)
What on Earth...

Others: What's
the matter?

Lugg: There's
a huge alien
swinging from planet
to planet.

Dekko: Don't worry!
It's only Starzan!

▷ STARDATE 000.021

Medical records show that Glich has come down with a very sore throat after eating some aluminium foil. Suspect tinsel-itis.

▷ STARDATE 000.022

EXTRACT FROM VOICE RECORDER

Glich: I think I'll take up badminton.
Lugg: Can't! The space shuttle's broken again.

▷ STARDATE 000.023

Lugg was surprised when the *ZS Rambler's* computer showed that they were heading for a part of the universe made entirely of salt water. After consulting his *Tough Guide to the Universe*, Zorb told her it was a new Galax-sea!

▷ STARDATE 000.024

Command from Lugg: Fill number two tank with custard and jelly.

Computer query: Please explain reason for command.

Lugg: I want to go a trifle faster.

▷ STARDATE 000.025

Command from Glich: Fill number four engine with fish fingers.

Computer query: Please explain reason for request.

Glich: I want to fly over Saturn and get a bird's eye view.

STARDATE 000.026

Report received from passing spacecraft that it had flown over a planet full of kangaroos. *Tough Guide to the Universe* identified it as Mars-upial.

STARDATE 000.027

Zorb: I've never seen such a grubby looking planet.
Lugg: Idiot! You've got your thumb over the telescope lens.

STARDATE 000.028

Ship's space observation cameras picked up a yellow spacecraft running away from a reported war zone.
Noted in log as an Unidentified Fleeing Object.

Dekko reported seeing a forty-foot long creature thought to have been extinct on Earth for millions of years, following *ZS Rambler*. It turned out to be a dino-saucer.

When passing Planet Robotia, the following signal was received:

▷ **Signal:** All our robots' batteries are flat. Can you help?

◁ **Reply:** Yes, but I'm afraid we'll have to charge you.

After charging the robots' batteries, the following signal was received:

▷ **Signal:** Other robots say I'm mad. Please advise.

◁ **Reply:** Just tell them you have a screw loose.

What's that knocking?

No, it's not the Rambler's *engine*, for a change. It's a selection of Lugg's and the others' favourite Knock! Knock! jokes.

Knock! Knock!
Who's there?
Lettuce!
Lettuce who?

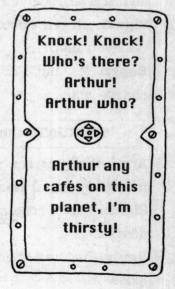

Lettuce get the *Rambler* started and get the heck out of here!

Knock! Knock!
Who's there?
Arthur!
Arthur who?

Arthur any cafés on this planet, I'm thirsty!

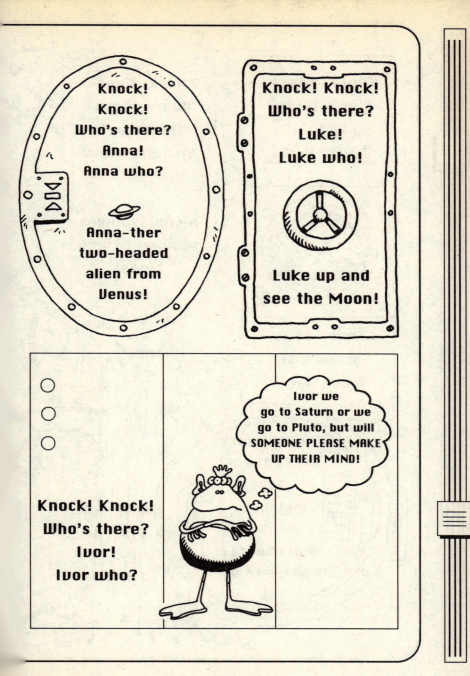

Knock! Knock!
Who's there?
Anna!
Anna who?

Anna-ther
two-headed
alien from
Venus!

Knock! Knock!
Who's there?
Luke!
Luke who!

Luke up and
see the Moon!

Knock! Knock!
Who's there?
Ivor!
Ivor who?

Ivor we
go to Saturn or we
go to Pluto, but will
SOMEONE PLEASE MAKE
UP THEIR MIND!

Knock! Knock!
Who's there?
Emma!
Emma who?

Emma little green man from Mars!

Knock! Knock!
Who's there?
Nicholas!
Nicholas who?

Nicholas aliens shouldn't climb trees!

Knock! Knock!
Who's there?
Owl!
Owl who?

Owl aboard?
Then we're off!

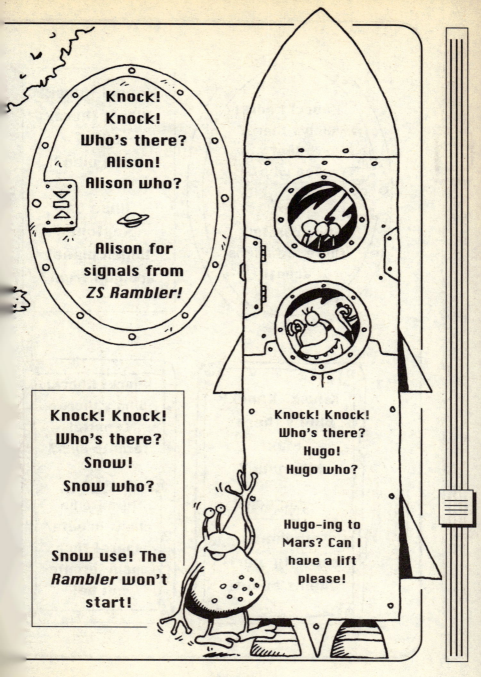

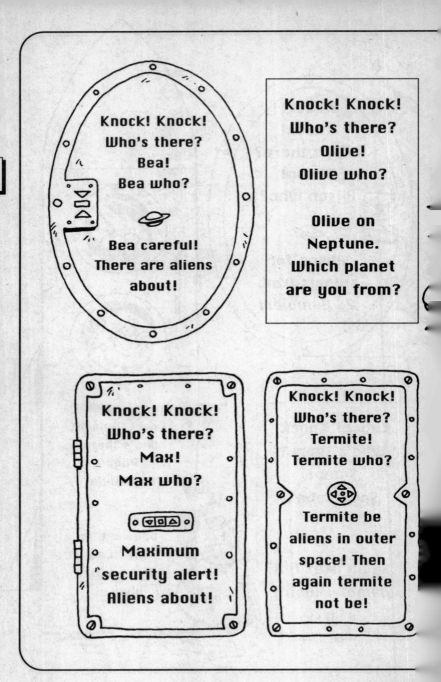

Knock! Knock!
Who's there?
Bea!
Bea who?

Bea careful!
There are aliens
about!

Knock! Knock!
Who's there?
Olive!
Olive who?

Olive on
Neptune.
Which planet
are you from?

Knock! Knock!
Who's there?
Max!
Max who?

Maximum
security alert!
Aliens about!

Knock! Knock!
Who's there?
Termite!
Termite who?

Termite be
aliens in outer
space! Then
again termite
not be!

Knock! Knock!
Who's there?
Harry!
Harry who?

Harry up and get out
of here. There's
a big, fat, hairy alien
just behind us!

Knock!
Knock!
Who's there?
Adair!
Adair who?

Adair you to
go and
pat that
big hairy
alien on the
head!

She's a technical genius, and when it comes to jokes, she's pretty hot, too!

How may ears does Captain Kirk have?

○ *Three — a left ear, a right ear and a final frontier!*

Lugg: What's three metres long, covered in purple hair and has eight legs?

Zorb: I don't know! What's three metres long, covered in purple hair and has eight legs?

Lugg: I don't know either. But it's crawling up your back!

What's ugly, lives on Mars and is very blue?

○ *An alien choking on its lunch!*

Lugg: How do the creatures on Star System Pisces catch fish?

Zorb: I don't know. How do the creatures on Star System Pisces catch fish?

Lugg: They breathe on them!

Zorb: How does breathing catch fish?

Lugg: Never heard of baited breath?

Why did Lugg take a ruler to bed with her?

○ *She wanted to see how long she would sleep!*

What happened when Lugg went on a crash diet?

○ *She went to a scrap yard for dinner every night...*

What's the difference between an alien
from Jupiter and an alien from Saturn?

◯ *About 200,000,000 miles!*

▶ **Lugg:** Why does dreaming about football
make you late for duty, Zorb?

Zorb: Because we played extra time!

▶ **Dekko:** That girl from Planet Grugg
just rolled her eyes at me.

Lugg: Well roll them right back,
she might need them!

Why did the alien take his nose apart?

◯ *To see what made it run!*

Lugg: When I was at school I swallowed fifty pence every day.

Zorb: Why?

Lugg: Because it was my dinner money!

What sort of pills do two-headed aliens take?

○ *Aspirins! They're good for splitting headaches!*

Lugg: My new boyfriend is one of twins.

Zorb: Can you tell them apart?

Lugg: Of course. His sister hasn't got a beard!

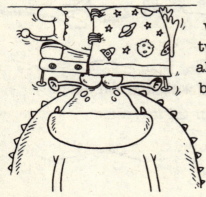

How do you know when there's a twenty-foot tall alien under your bed?

○ *Your nose touches the ceiling!*

Why did the alien call his pet dog 'Fog'?
○ *Because he was grey and thick.*

How can you tell if an alien has been in the fridge?
○ *The toothmarks on the door!*

What would you do with a green alien?
○ *Put it in the sun till it ripens!*

What would you give an alien with food poisoning?

○ *Lots of room!*

Lugg: I've just met a Martian with the most lifelike glass eye I've ever seen.

Zorb: If it was so lifelike, how did you know it was artificial?

Lugg: It came out in conversation!

What's got two-heads, black scales, comes from Mars and bounces up and down?

○ *A Martian on a pogo-stick!*

Lugg: Heard about the alien who lost a hand when his spaceship crashed on Saturn?

Glich: Poor thing! What did he do?

Lugg: He hitched a lift to Earth and went to an Oxfam shop.

Glich: An Oxfam Shop?

Lugg: Yes! He'd heard they're the best second-hand shops in the Universe!

Did you hear about the Martians whose spaceship landed in a swamp?

○ *They got bogged down in their work!*

What should you do if an alien runs in through your front door?

○ *Run out through your back door!*

Why did the alien knit itself three socks?

○ *Because it grew another foot!*

His memory may sometimes let him down, but when it comes to jokes, Dekko can be relied upon to remember some of the best.

An Earthling, mad about cars,
Went into several bars.
He got a bit tiddly,
Found steering so fiddly,
That he ended up driving to Mars!

Dekko: What do you get if you cross a Martian with a pair of glasses?

Zorb: I don't know. What do you get if you cross a Martian with a pair of glasses?

Dekko: An alien that keeps on making a spectacle of itself!

Dekko: What do mad aliens have for Christmas dinner?

Lugg: I don't know, but no doubt you're going to tell me!

Dekko: Duck!

Lugg: Why duck?

Dekko: Because there's a spaceship heading straight for you!

Why did the alien have a lid on top of his head?

☒ *He was forever changing his mind!*

Lugg: Seriously, though. Do crazy aliens really have duck for Christmas dinner?

Dekko: Yup!

Lugg: Why?

Dekko: Because they're quackers!

How can you tell if aliens from Saturn have been in your bathroom?

☒ *From the rings on the bath.*

What was the
Martian
wandering
around
Saturn
looking at
a map of
Jupiter?

☒ *Lost!*

Dekko: What's the capital of Mars?

Zorb: Dunno! What IS the capital of Mars?

Dekko: M!

What washing powder did the
hairless alien use?

☒ *Bald automatic!*

Dekko: When we landed on Earth we went for a tramp in the woods.

Lugg: Enjoy it?

Dekko: We did! I don't think the tramp was too keen though...

Dekko: Heard the one about the Earthling who fell in love with an alien?

Zorb: Yes! It was love at first fright!

Why did the crew of the *ZS Rambler* eat a sofa and three chairs for pudding one night?

⊠ *They all had a suite tooth!*

Dekko: Did you hear about the one-eyed alien who set itself up as a driving instructor?

Lugg: No! What about it?

Dekko: It went bust!

Lugg: Why'd it go bust?

Dekko: It only had one pupil...

What do you call an alien couple with seven children?

☒ *Mummy and Daddy!*

▶ **Dekko:** Did you hear about the skinny alien with six-inch nails?

Glich: No, but I've a funny feeling you're going to tell me about it.

Dekko: If you picked her up by the feet she made a terrific back-scratcher.

 Where do aliens who want to be movie stars move to?

☒ *Planet Hollywood*

Where does a three-headed alien with the body of a horse and the legs of a rhino sleep?

☒ *Anywhere it wants!*

▷ **Dekko:** I've just heard about a planet where the aliens have long, hairy arms, enormous moustaches and long beards, and worse of all, they all smoke cigars.

Zorb: Really?

Dekko: Yes! And the men are just as bad!

▷ **Dekko:** Did you hear about the alien who was made of jelly?

Lugg: Don't think so.

Dekko: He entered the 100 metres sprint and when the starter said, 'Get Set!' he did!

Dekko: Did you hear about the alien who changed into an onion?

Lugg: No, what about it?

Dekko: It was in a dreadful pickle!

Glich: I did hear about the alien who changed into a dumpling, though.

Dekko: Poor thing!

Glich: Yes! It was in a terrible stew!

What do you call an alien whose UFO lands in the sea?

☒ *Bob!*

What do you get if a ten-tonne alien sits on your piano?

☒ *A flat note!*

Dekko: Heard about the alien who sent his picture to a lonely hearts club?

Zorb: What about him?

Dekko: They sent it back saying they weren't that lonely!

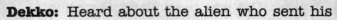

Dekko: How do you keep a stupid alien in suspense?

Lugg: No idea! How do you keep a stupid alien in suspense?

Dekko: I'll tell you tomorrow.

An alien who went to Dundee,
Fell over and fractured a knee.
Broke twelve of its toes,
Four wrists and a nose,
Then died when 'twas stung by a bee!

A thing from a planet called Ghent,
Had a nose that was quite badly bent.
One day, I suppose,
It followed its nose,
And nobody knew where
it went!

A Moonman who landed in Leeds,
Swallowed a packet of seeds.
Within half-an-hour,
Its nose grew a flower,
And its back was a riot of weeds.

An alien lass known as Beck,
Could wrap all her legs round her neck.
But then she forgot
How to untie the knot,
And now she's a highly strung wreck!

A lazy young alien, Fred,
Enjoyed eating soup while in bed.
One morning it spilt,
All over his quilt.
So he ate all the
bedclothes instead!

Poor Glich! Someone said she was plain.
So she dressed herself up. But in vain.
Her ringlets and bangles,
Sparkled like spangles.
But she rusted when caught in the rain!

A Martian whose friends called him Ned,
Had eyes at the back of his head.
When asked where he's going,
'I've no way of knowing.
But I know where I've been to!' he said.

A ten-year-old alien called Ned,
Ate crisp after crisp in his bed.
His mum said, 'Look, son.
This is really no fun.
Why don't you eat people instead?'

They come from Venus and Mars,
From places beyond all the stars.
They're red, pink and green,
But they've never been seen.
They're aliens playing guitars!

An alien was strolling hand in hand across the Moon with his girlfriend. 'Look darling,' he sighed, gazing upwards. 'It's a full Earth tonight.'

★ GIGGLE

Glich: I know who lives on the dark side of the Moon.

Lugg: Who?

Glich: People who don't pay their electricity bill!

▼ ★ GIGGLE

Lugg: I've just heard they've opened a new restaurant on the Moon.

Zorb: You don't want to go there.

Lugg: Why not?

Zorb: Well, the food's alright, but there's no atmosphere!

▼ ★ GIGGLE

Zorb: There's something I've always wanted to know about astronauts from Earth.

Glich: What's that?

Zorb: Well, if they're so smart, how come they always count backwards!

What time is it when a three-tonne alien lands on your cat?

★ *Time to get a new cat!*

How does an alien count to thirty-one?

★ *He takes off his left shoe!*

What does a boy alien call a girl alien with three heads, brown fur and a scaly face?

★ *Cute!*

'Hurry up and make my sandwiches,' a Martian schoolboy demanded. 'I'll be late for school!'

'Don't rush me,' snapped his mother. 'I've only got three pairs of hands!'

Two Venusians in London landed their spaceship in front of a set of traffic lights.

'She's mine,' said one of the aliens.

'I saw her first!'

'Maybe,' said the second. 'But it's me she's winking at!'

An alien landed on Earth in a big city and just as he clambered out of his spaceship, a dustbin lorry roared by, and a rubbish bin fell off and rolled towards him.

'Stop, Lady,' cried the alien. 'You've dropped your purse!'

▼ ★ GIGGLE

Dekko: Heard about the creature from Planet Mungo who landed on Earth and was run over by a steam roller?

Lugg: No! What happened to him?

Dekko: His doctor told him to lie flat on his back for a month!

In a Las Vegas casino, someone playing a fruit machine hit the jackpot. As coin after coin cascaded to the floor, a visiting alien went up to the fruit machine, patted it on the head and said, 'Are you taking anything for that cold?'

What do get if you cross an alien with a computer?

★ *A four-headed creature with an IQ of 1,000!*

What's the best place to talk to an angry alien?

★ *From as far away as possible!*

Why did Glich put her CD player in the deep freeze?

★ *She wanted to listen to really cool music!*

What's the difference between an alien and a digestive biscuit?

★ *You can't dunk an alien in your tea!*

▼ ★ GIGGLE

Glich: My new boyfriend's named after his father.

Lugg: What's his name?

Glich: Dad!

What did it say on the metallic alien's gravestone?

★ *Rust in piece!*

▼ ★ GIGGLE

Lugg: Did you know that the inhabitants of Planet Plutonia eat nothing but little bits of sharp metal?

Zorb: Sounds like a staple diet to me!

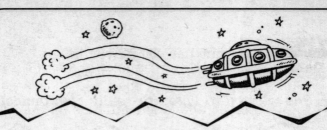

Why did the hungry man-eating alien stop at a transport café on the M1?

★ *It heard they served lorry drivers!*

Why is a cold germ stronger than the strongest alien?

★ *Because it can bring an alien to its sneeze!*

▼ ★ GIGGLE

Patient: Doctor! Doctor! I think I'm an alien!

Doctor: How long have you felt like this?

Patient: Since I got here from Jupiter!

▼ ★ GIGGLE

First alien: I took a trip on Mars last year.

Second alien: Oh dear! I hope you didn't hurt yourself!

Dekko: Did you hear the joke about the alien who could float forty metres above the surface of the Earth?

Glich: No, tell me about it.

Dekko: Don't think I'll bother: it's way above your head!

Zorb: Did you know that the inhabitants of Planet Bigdigita can write with their toes?

Glich: Great for making footnotes!

Why can't you put an alien in a sandwich?

★ *It would be too heavy to lift!*

DEKKO'S TOP TONGUE TWISTERS

With his enormously long tongue, Dekko finds most twisters a breeze, but even he's had trouble with some of these ones. See how you do!

Peter Piper picked a peck of pickled pepper;
Did Peter Piper pick a peck of pickled pepper?
If Peter Piper picked a peck of pickled pepper,
Where's the peck of pickled pepper Pig from
   Pluto picked?

The Leith police dismisseth us.

The sixth sheik's sixth sheep is as the sixth sheik is!

She sells sea-shells on the sea shore;
The shells that she sells are sea-shells I'm sure.
So if she sells sea-shells on the sea shore,
I'm sure that the shells she sells are
   sea shore shells.

Careful Katie cooked a crisp and
   crinkly cabbage;
Did careful Katie cook a crisp and
   crinkly cabbage?
If careful Katie cooked a crisp and
   crinkly cabbage,
Where's the crisp and crinkly cabbage
   careful Katie cooked?

Beth believes
thieves seize skis.

Why did the chicken stow away
on the *ZS Rambler*?

★ *It wanted to eggs-plore outer space.*

Why did Glich want to paint the
ZS Rambler red?

★ *She wanted a tomato saucer!*

Why did Glich want a tomato saucer?

★ *So that no other ship could ketchup
with it!*

What happened when Lugg and Dekko entered the three-legged race in the Intergalactic Olympics?

They didn't win, but they got a constellation prize!

What do you call a little green man with two heads who comes from Brisbane?

 An Austr-alien!

▶ **Alien pilot:** Intergalactic flight 1VAB1GBUM approaching Planet Dispepsiacola. Landing instructions, please.

IG Control: Your height and position please?

Alien pilot: I'm four metres tall and I'm sitting in the cockpit. Now can I have landing instructions?!

Alien 1: My new baby is the spitting image of me!

Alien 2: Never mind, as long as it's healthy!

Lugg: Did you hear about the body snatchers from Planet X?

Dekko: No! What about them?

Lugg: Better not tell you, you might get carried away!

Why did the baby alien put his father in the freezer?

⭐ *Because he wanted frozen pop!*

▼ **OUT OF THIS WORLD!**

Why did the astronaut go for a walk in space?

Because he missed the bus!

What do you get if you cross a grumpy man with a spaceship?

⭐ *A moan rocket!*

Alien 1: My boyfriend took me to the movies last night – we saw *The Creature From The Sweaty Swamp!*

Alien 2: What was he like?

Alien 1: About ten feet tall with three eyes and one big ear on the top of his head.

Alien 1: Not your boyfriend! The Creature From The Sweaty Swamp!

How do you greet a two-headed alien?

⭐ *Hi! Hi! How are you? How are you?*

Why do men from Mars have green ears and long red heads?

⭐ *So they can hide in the rhubarb patch!*

▼ **OUT OF THIS WORLD!**

What do big aliens do with asteroids?

 *Play marbles with them!*

What's purple, covered in hair and shakes all the time?

⭐ *An alien with a pneumatic drill!*

Did you hear about the alien who had four pongy feet and bad breath?

⭐ *It had foot and mouth disease!*

How do you get an alien in the back of a Mini?

⭐ *Open the door and push back the driver's seat?*

What do you call a six-metre tall alien in a phone box?

⭐ *Stuck!*

What would happen if a three-metre tall alien sat in front of you at the movies?

⭐ *You'd miss most of the movie!*

What do you get if you cross an alien with a watchdog?

⭐ *Terrified postmen!*

What's mad and orbits the Moon?

 A loony module!

Did you hear about the alien who turned into a frog?

⭐ *He'd been playing too much croquet!*

Did you hear about the alien with perfect eyesight?

⭐ *It had 20-20-20-20 vision!*

Dekko: Heard about the alien who was caught speeding?

Lugg: Yes! Wasn't he fined £50 and dismantled for six months?

Dekko: Heard the one about the two computers who had a baby?

Zorb: No! What about it?

Dekko: Its first word was, 'Data!'

Suitor: Glich, will you marry me?

Glich: No, but I'll always admire your good taste!

What's red and stringy and travels at the speed of light?

⭐ *A bowl of Spaghetti Bolognese in a UFO!*

How do you send a baby alien to sleep?

⭐ *Rocket!*

An alien whose friends called him Bill,
Always ate more than his fill.
He thought, 'Does it matter,
That I'm getting much fatter?'
Then he burst. Doesn't that make you ill?

What do you get if you cross a snowball with a sharp-toothed alien?

☒ *Frost bite!*

What do you get if you cross a prehistoric alien with a man having a doze?

☒ *A dinosnore!*

What do you get if you cross a clumsy alien with a biscuit?

☒ *Crumbs!*

What do you get if you cross a Martian with an octopus?

☒ *A heavily armed alien!*

What do you get if you cross a cow with an alien who believes in Spiritualism?

☒ *A message from the Udder Side of the Universe!*

What do you get if you cross an angry alien with a tiger?

⊠ *Exhausted from running as fast as you can to get the heck out of there!*

What do you get if you cross a dog with a giraffe?

⊠ *An animal that barks at low-flying UFOs!*

And what do you get if you cross an alien spacecraft with a baby?

⊠ *An Unidentified Crying Object!*

What do you get if you cross an alien spacecraft with a shopoholic?

⊠ *An Unidentified Buying Object!*

It's a dog's life on the ZS Rambler, but a fun one too!

What happened when Rover went to the flea circus?

He walked off with the show!

Why does Rover spend most of his time chasing his tail?

He's trying to make both ends meet!

What goes 'Woof! Woof! Tick! Tock!'

Rover when he's on watch!

What did Zorb say when Rover
got lost in space?

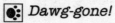 *Dawg-gone!*

Zorb: We've lost
Rover.

Glich: Why don't
we put an
ad in the
Alien News?

Zorb: Don't be silly. Rover
can't read!

Young Zorb: Mum! Can I have a puppy
for Christmas?

Zorb's Mum: No! You're having turkey
like everyone else!

What would you do if you found Rover in
your bed?

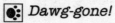 *Sleep somewhere else if you know
what's good for you!*

What fish does Rover enjoy chasing?

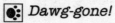 *Catfish!*

Lugg: Zorb! Stop pulling Rover's tail!

Zorb: That's not fair! It's Rover who is doing the pulling!

Why did Zorb want to put Rover in the lunar-tic asylum?

Because he was barking mad!

When the *ZS Rambler* landed on Planet Hollywood, Zorb took Rover to the cinema. During a break in the film, the creature behind Zorb tapped him on the shoulder and said, 'I'm surprised to see that your dog seems to be actually enjoying the movie.' 'So am I,' said Zorb. 'He hated the book!'

What do you call an alien dog with four rows of razor-sharp teeth?

Anything it wants you to!

How does the vet
examine Rover's teeth?

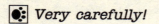 *Very carefully!*

'Doctor! Doctor! Rover's just swallowed
a pen.'
'I'll be there as soon as I can.'
'What shall I do till you get here?'
'Use a pencil!'

Zorb: Why was the dachshund sitting in
the frying pan?

Lugg: I don't know, but you're probably
going to tell me!

Zorb: Because it heard someone say it
was a sausage dog!

Glich: Doctor! Doctor! I've got this
strange feeling that Rover is
taking me over.

Doctor: Sit down and tell me about it.

Glich: I can't. I'm not allowed to sit on
the furniture.

Lugg: Heck, Zorb! Every time you play the violin Rover howls like a banshee.

Zorb: I know!

Lugg: Well, couldn't you play something he doesn't know!

 Alien: Is Rover fond of children?

Zorb: Yes, but he prefers biscuits!

What did Rover say when he sat on a sheet of sandpaper?

 Ruff!

What did Rover say when Lugg took the book he was chewing away from him?

 'You've taken the words right out of my mouth!'

 And why did Lugg want to call Rover 'Ginger?'

 Because he snaps!

'That dog is bone idle,' said Glich, pointing at Rover.

'What do you mean?' asked Dekko.

'When I was watering the plants yesterday, it never lifted a leg to help me!'

'There's only one thing I dislike about Rover,' said Glich one day.

'What's that?' asked Lugg.

'The way he hides under the bed when we go through an electrical storm.'

'He's just a bit frightened,' said Lugg. 'Where's the harm in that?'

'There isn't enough room for me!'

 Lugg: Did you know there's a Dog Star!

Zorb: You cannot be Sirius!

THE ZOOMASTER

Wherever the ZS Rambler goes, the Intergalactic Zoo, with its hold full of alien creatures, is not far behind. And the Zoomaster and Pecksniff Blabber are not far behind in the joke stakes, either. For they have a monstrous sense of humour!

What do you get if you cross a monster with a hamster?

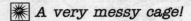 *A very messy cage!*

On what day do monsters eat people?

※ *Chewsday!*

What always goes in front of the Loch Ness Monster?

✳ *The Loch Ness Monster's head!*

What did the Loch Ness Monster say to his friend?

✳ *Hi! Long time no sea!*

Why did the monster cross the road?

✳ *He was on his way to a fancy dress party disguised as a chicken!*

Zoomaster: I must go and welcome that three-headed monster from Planet Zegovia.

Pecksniff: What are you going to say to it?

Zoomaster: Hello! Hello! Hello!

How do you communicate with a monster
that lives on the bottom of the sea?

※ *Easy! Drop him a line!*

What do female monsters do at parties?

※ *Keep an eye out for edible bachelors!*

What do you get if
you cross a monster
with a skunk?

※ *An ugly smell!*

What did the monster order in
Macdonalds?

※ *A big waiter.*

Pecksniff: Why does the Monster from
Mongrovia have such thick fur?

Zoomaster: Because he'd look stupid in a
plastic mac!

 **Pecksniff:** Zoomaster, the monster from Planet X has a sore throat.

Zoomaster: Give it something to gargoyle!

Why didn't the monster eat the chocolate alarm clock?

Too time-consuming!

How do you know if there's a monster in the shower?

You can't close the shower curtain!

What did the monster say when he saw a train full of people?

'Great! A chew-chew train!'

What should you do if a monster joins you on a picnic?

✳ *Let it sit wherever it wants and give it the best sandwiches!*

What's hairy, dangerous and has eight wheels?

✳ *A monster on roller blades!*

Pecksniff: There's something making a funny noise in the Zoo, Zoomaster.

Zoomaster: What noise?

Pecksniff: 99-clonk! 99-clonk!

Zoomaster: Oh, it's that centipede with the wooden leg.

Pecksniff: Zoomaster, the spiders from Planet Arachnida have got into the dynamite hold!

Zoomaster: Blast!

Pecksniff: Look, Zoomaster. The snails in that cage are having a fight.

Zoomaster: Let's leave them to slug it out.

Who won the Miss Monster competition on Mars?

✳ *No one!*

What book did all the fleas in the *Intergalactic Zoo* read?

✳ *The 'Itch-hikers Guide to the Galaxy'!*

GLICH'S GROANERS

There are chuckles galore when that queen of cosmic comedians, Glich, tells some of her favourite jokes.

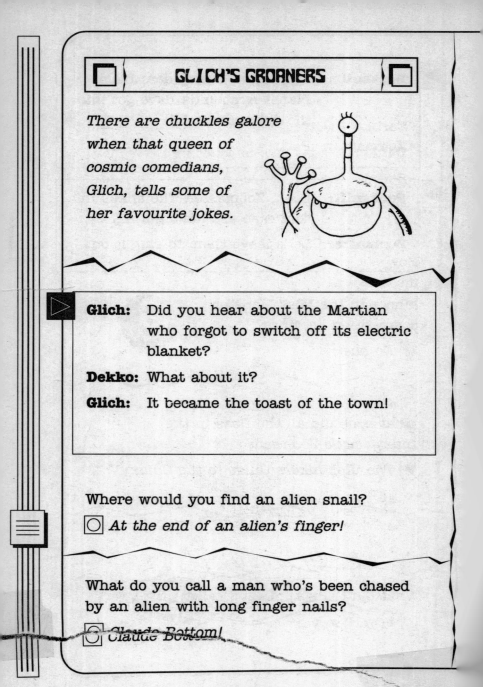

Glich: Did you hear about the Martian who forgot to switch off its electric blanket?

Dekko: What about it?

Glich: It became the toast of the town!

Where would you find an alien snail?

◯ *At the end of an alien's finger!*

What do you call a man who's been chased by an alien with long finger nails?

◯ *Claude Bottom!*

Dekko: On which side of his head does a Martian have most eyes?

Zorb: On the...

Dekko: Whose joke is this?

Zorb: Sor-ry!

Dekko: On the outside!

How do you tell a friendly alien from a mean one?

☐ *If it's friendly, you'll be able to tell your friends about it!*

What did the stupid alien call its pet tiger?

☐ *Spot!*

How can you tell the difference between an alien and a goldfish?

○ *Ever tried getting an alien into a goldfish bowl?!*

What do astronauts eat immediately after take-off?

○ *High tea!*

What did the alien do after it had all its teeth pulled?

○ *Licked the dentist to death!*

How do you get a baby astronaut to sleep?

○ *Rocket!*

Glich: I want that bag to go to Venus, that one to Mars and the third one to end up on Saturn.

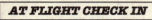

Ticket alien: We can't do that!

Glich: Why not? That's what happened the last time I flew with you!

Zorb: Can you telephone from the *ZS Rambler*?

Glich: I'd be very worried about my eyesight if I couldn't!

Lugg: What does ET stand for?

Glich: He's been sitting for so long, his bum is sore!

What's the time when a UFO lands in your back garden?

◯ Time to get the heck out of there!

Glich: How does an alien shave her legs?

Zorb: How should I know?

Glich: With a laser blade!

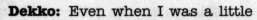

Dekko: Even when I was a little boy I wanted to work on a spaceship!

Glich: You mean you were born with high hopes?

Why was the *ZS Rambler's* computer so thin?

○ It hadn't had a byte for ages!

Why did the *ZS Rambler's* cat sit on top of the ship's computer?

○ *To keep an eye on the mouse!*

Why did Glich's computer go on the blink?

⊙ *It had a slipped disk!*

Why are aliens so forgetful?

⊙ *Because everything you tell them goes in one ear and straight out of the others!*

▷ **Glich:** Do you really find me attractive, Dekko?

Dekko: I do! I do!

Glich: Then whisper something sweet in my ear.

Dekko: Lemon Meringue Pie! Lemon Meringue Pie!

▷ **Glich's friend:** I got a beautiful Burmese cat for my boyfriend.

Glich: I wish I could barter like you!

*Before he goes to bed each
night, Zorb writes up his
diary. Here's what he wrote
one March, a couple of
light years ago.*

1ST MARCH ○

I'm going off Glich! I asked her if she
would ever punish someone for something
they hadn't done. She said, 'No!', so I told
her I hadn't done the washing-up. So what
does she do? She puts me on washing-up
duty for a month!

2ND MARCH ○

   The heating went off. Lugg went into the
hold and came back with two bits of wood.
'Does anyone know how to make a fire
with two sticks?' she asked.

'Sure,' I said. 'Make sure that one of them is a match!'

3RD MARCH ◯

My pen ran out.
Ran after it!

4TH MARCH ◯

ZS Rambler's ladder was stolen.

If not returned by tomorrow, Lugg said further steps will be taken.

5TH MARCH ◯

Flew over Alaska and saw lots of Eskimos.
I think they're God's frozen people!

6TH MARCH ◯

Asked Glich if she had heard the joke about the dirty shirt.

'No!' she said.

'That one's on you,'
I said.

*(Back on washing-up
duty. It's SO unfair!)*

7TH MARCH ○

Dekko asked what we would get if we plotted a course 1.15 degrees north for half a light year, 11.00 degrees south-east for six deci-seconds, then went straight ahead until we got to Caspia.

I thought for a moment, then said, 'A headache!'

8TH MARCH ○

Landed on Planet Fairy Tale for the football. Cinderella's team should have won, but she kept running away from the ball...

9TH MARCH ○

Decided to play in the Mars Open Golf tournament and took two pairs of trousers with me in case I got a hole in one.

10TH MARCH ○

Asked the doctor if he could cure my spots.

'Can't say,' he said. 'I never make rash promises!'

11TH MARCH ⟡

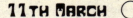

'How do you feel today?' asked Lugg.

'Same as usual,' I answered. 'With my hands!'

12TH MARCH ⟡

Had to go to the dentist and found him with a sketchpad in his hand.

'What are you doing?' I asked.

'Drawing teeth!'

13TH MARCH ⟡

Glich told me she had flat feet and asked what she should do about them.

Suggested she try a bicycle pump!

15TH MARCH ○

Couldn't sleep last night until I lay on the edge of the bed.

Soon dropped off!

16TH MARCH ○

'How did you find the weather on Saturn when you were there?' asked Lugg.

'I just slipped outside,' I said. 'And there it was!'

17TH MARCH ○

ZS Rambler passed two angels sitting on a cloud. Opened a porthole and shouted, 'Halo!'

18TH MARCH ○

Flew over a city populated by cows.

'Where's that?' asked Lugg.

'Moo York,' I replied.

19TH MARCH ⃝

Flew over a safari park on
Earth.

'Name ten animals that
live in Africa,' challenged Glich.

'Easy,' I said. 'Nine elephants and a lion.'

20TH MARCH ⃝

'I'm glad I didn't become an archaeologist,'
I said to Dekko at breakfast.

'Why's that?' he asked.

'Because,' I replied, 'if I had my life
would be in ruins!'

21ST MARCH ⃝

Think I may give up this job and go to
work in a bank. There's more money in it!

22ND MARCH ⃝

Swallowed the clock by mistake.

How alarming!

(Tomorrow's
Alien Fool's Day:
watch out everyone...)

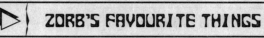

ZORB'S FAVOURITE THINGS

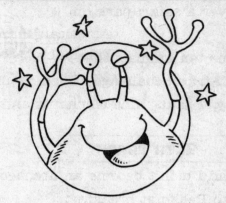

★ FAVOURITE MOVIE ★
The Texas Chain Saw Mars-acre

★ FAVOURITE BOOK ★
The Big Bang Theory by Dinah Mite

★ FAVOURITE POP GROUP ★
Gerry and the Space Makers

★ FAVOURITE TELEVISION PROGRAMME ★
Blast-off the Summer Wine

★ FAVOURITE JOKE ★

Can a Native American change a lightbulb?
How!

★ FAVOURITE FOOD ★

Fish'n' Chips (nuclear fission chips)

★ FAVOURITE SHAMPOO ★

Wash and Glow

★ FAVOURITE COLOUR ★

Corduroy

★ FAVOURITE SPORTSMAN ★

Anyone who plays in ghouls

★ FAVOURITE SCHOOL SUBJECT ★

Arts and spacecrafts

★ TOP HORROR MOVIE ★

Close Encounters of the Cursed Kind

★ TOP BOOK ★

Growing Pot Plants on Pluto
by Hardy Annual

★ TOP GAME ★

Moon-opoly

★ TOP TELEVISION PROGRAMME ★

Countdown

★ TOP JOKE ★

How many idiots does it take to
change alight bulb?

*Two! One to take the old one out and
put the new one in, and one to switch
off the gas, just in case!*

★ TOP FOOD ★

Mars-malade

★ TOP DRINK ★

Current juice (electric current juice)

★ TOP MOTTO ★

If at first you don't succeed,
fly, fly and fly again

★ TOP ANIMAL ★

Any Mars-upial

★ TOP SWEET ★

Apollo mints

★ BEST MOVIE ★

Escape from the Prison Planet (but it
hasn't been released yet...)

★ BEST BOOK ★

Get Rich Quick by Robin Banks

★ BEST MUSIC ★

The Planets

★ BEST TELEVISION PROGRAMME ★

Changing ZOOMS

★ BEST JOKE ★

What does the Queen do when a light bulb
needs changing in Buckingham Palace?

Moves to Windsor Castle!

★ BEST LAMB DISH ★

Rum baa-baas

★ BEST HISTORICAL CHARACTER ★

Davie Rocket, King of the Final Frontier

★ BEST ANIMALS ★

Hens (battery hens)

★ BEST LULLABY ★

Rocket Bye Baby

★ BEST FILM STAR ★

Tom Cruise-Missile

★ ACEST MOVIE ★
Star-zan of the Apes

★ ACEST BOOKS ★
The Wind from Outer Space by Rufus
Blownoff

★ ACEST FAIRY TALE ★
Beauty and the Beep

★ ACEST CITY ★
Electri-city

★ ACEST JOKE ★

Who changes the lightbulbs in Windsor Castle?

'My Husband and I...'

★ ACEST DRINK ★

Tea – gravi-tea

★ ACEST MEAL ★

A light snack – an electric light snack

★ ACEST TV CHANNEL ★

Beep! Beep! C2

★ ACEST LEADER ★

Robot the Bruce

★ ACEST PET ★

Rover, his astro-mutt

Have a good giggle with the other joke books
in this series. They're sometimes wacky,
often silly but always worth sharing!

And delve into the diaries!
Follow the daily shenanigans in the lives of
the Gory vampire family, pirate Captain Ben
Blunder and alien traveller Zorb Zork and their
friends. Then bone-up on vampires, pirates and
aliens in the fascinating Spotters Guides.

But make sure you don't miss vampires,
pirates and aliens on your televisions!